INVESTIGATING THE UNKNOWN

Discovering PAST LIVES

Carl R. Green and William R. Sanford

Enslow Publishers, Inc.
40 Industrial Road
Box 398
Berkeley Heights, NJ 07922
USA

http://www.enslow.com

Original edition published as *Recalling Past Lives* in 1993.

Library of Congress Cataloging-in-Publication Data

Green, Carl R.
    Discovering past lives / Carl R. Green and William R. Sanford ; illustrated by Gerald Kelley.
      p. cm. — (Investigating the unknown)
    Originally published: Recalling past lives. 1993.
    Includes bibliographical references and index.
    Summary: "Explores past lives, including real-life incidents of people remembering past lives, age regression and hypnosis, reincarnation, and a scientific study of past lives"—Provided by publisher.
    ISBN 978-0-7660-3818-9
    1. Reincarnation—Juvenile literature. I. Sanford, William R. (William Reynolds), 1927– II. Kelley, Gerald, ill. III. Green, Carl R. Recalling past lives. IV. Title.
    BL515.G74 2012
    133.901'35—dc22   2010045202

Paperback ISBN 978-1-59845-308-9

Printed in China
052011 Leo Paper Group, Heshan City, Guangdong, China

10 9 8 7 6 5 4 3 2 1

To Our Readers: We have done our best to make sure all Internet addresses in this book were active and appropriate when we went to press. However, the author and the publisher have no control over and assume no liability for the material available on those Internet sites or on other Web sites they may link to. Any comments or suggestions can be sent by e-mail to comments@enslow.com or to the address on the back cover.

Illustration Credits: The Art Archive / Alfredo Dagli Orti, p. 30; © Bubbles Photolibrary / Alamy, p. 28; © Hemis / Alamy, p. 13; Library of Congress, p. 15 (right); © 2011 Photos.com, a division of Getty Images, pp. 14, 15 (left), 35, 40; Shutterstock.com, pp. 1, 4, 6, 42; Courtesy of Special Collections, Occidental College, p. 18; © Warner Bros. / Everett Collection, p. 41.

Original Illustrations: © 2010 Gerald Kelley, www.geraldkelley.com, pp. 8, 10, 17, 20, 22, 24, 27, 32, 38.

Cover Illustration: O. Burriel / Photo Researchers, Inc. (Abstract image of a woman in a hypnotic trance).

Contents

Authors' Note

Thanks to science, many of nature's great mysteries have been solved. Do you want to know more about earthquakes or earthworms? There's probably an expert somewhere who can answer most of your questions. But wouldn't this be a boring world if we knew all there is to know? Perhaps that's why people want to believe that the mind does possess mysterious powers.

In this series, you'll learn about these mysteries of the unknown:

- *The Mystery of Fortune-Telling*
- *Astonishing Mind Powers*
- *The Mysterious Secrets of Dreams*
- *Amazing Out-of-Body Experiences*
- *Discovering Past Lives*
- *Sensing the Unknown*

Do such mysteries truly exist? Some people say yes, others say no. Once you've studied both sides of the debate, you can decide for yourself. Along the way, keep one important thought in mind. In this field, it is often hard to separate the real from the fake. It pays to be skeptical when setting out to explore the mysteries of the unknown.

"Daddy, I'm Coming Home"

CHAPTER ONE

The Gupta family of Delhi, India, welcomed the birth of a son in 1956. At first, little Gopal seemed quite normal. Things changed when he began to talk.

One day, Mr. Gupta asked his son to pick up a glass. "I won't pick it up," the boy snapped. He said he was a high-born Brahmin. Members of the Brahmin caste, he added, do not do servants' work. Then Gopal flew into a rage and broke some of the glasses.

Mr. Gupta pressed his son for more facts. Gopal said he had once lived in a city a hundred miles away. He had owned a company that made medicines. The boy described the business, his house, and his family. Finally, Gopal said, he had fought with his brother. His death, he added, had come at the hands of that same brother.

At first, the Guptas laughed at the child's tale. A few years later, however, Mr. Gupta happened to go to the city Gopal had described. While there, he checked his son's story. To Mr. Gupta's surprise, the company did exist. The owner had been murdered by his brother. Soon after, some members of the dead man's family visited the Gupta home. Gopal greeted all of them by name. Then Gopal talked about matters that only a family member could know. The murder, he said, took place because he refused his spendthrift brother's demands for money.

Gopal Gupta throws a temper tantrum when his father tells him to pick up a glass. Gopal tells his family that he was born a Brahmin, a member of India's highest caste—and Brahmins did not do servants' work. Gopal then goes on to describe a past life in which he was a factory owner.

Gopal's strange behavior faded as time passed. Although he still claimed to be a Brahmin, he gradually adjusted to a simpler lifestyle. For their part, his "other family" did not forget him. They were convinced that he was their son, reborn in a new body.[1]

Many people expect stories of rebirth to come out of Asia. They know that eastern religions believe in reincarnation (rebirth in a new body). Cases like that of the Guptas, however, also take place in the West.

Useful Definitions

Researchers who study the mysteries of the mind have worked hard to define the terms used to discuss past lives. Here are a few of the key words:

age regression—To move back in time to discover past lives, often under hypnosis. During age regression, a person may claim to remember a past life in which he or she served as a Civil War soldier or as a Boston nurse.

cryptomnesia—The retrieval of memories that have been buried in the unconcious mind. Subjects are not aware that they have been exposed to the data contained in these memories.

déjà vu—A feeling of having already been in a certain place or having lived through a certain situation, even though you know it is not possible. People report that during a déjà vu experience they "know" what will happen next.

Past Lives Therapy (PLT)—A treatment in which hypnotists help relate current life problems to past-life traumas. For example, a person might conquer a phobic fear of fire after learning that a house fire caused his or her death in a past life.

reincarnation—The belief that one can be reborn in a new body or as a different form of life. A man might believe that he is the reincarnation of a woman who died in childbirth in the 1800s.

Born two years after her sister Winnie's death, Susan claims that she *is* Winnie. Given a box of crayons, she scrawls "WINNI" on the kitchen door. In time, her parents became convinced that Susan was Winnie reborn.

In 1961, Winnie Eastland was a happy six-year-old living in Idaho. She died that year when she was hit by a car. A few days later, her mother and her sister Sharon had similar dreams. Each dreamed that Winnie would return to them.

Two years later, Winnie's father paced a waiting room while his wife gave birth. Just before his daughter Susan was born, he thought he heard Winnie speak to him. "Daddy, I'm coming home," the voice said.

The real surprises began when Susan was two years old. She told her friends that she was six (Winnie's age at the time of her death). When she saw pictures of Winnie, she said, "That was me." Given a box of crayons, Susan wrote "WINNI" on the kitchen door.

The Eastlands found it easy to think that Winnie had returned. Susan recalled family jokes, picnics, friends, and trips. All of the events had taken place before she was born. Told of the case, researchers were skeptical. Didn't the Eastlands often talk about Winnie while Susan was in the room? The girl's "memories," they said, had to be based on clues picked up from the family. The Eastlands did not back down. They were certain that Winnie had been reborn in Susan's body.[2]

Skeptics are quick to write off stories like that of the Eastlands, but there is one fact they cannot deny. The debate over past lives is nearly as old as human culture.

A Belief That Spans the Ages

The belief that each of us lives many lives may have begun ten thousand years ago. In the New Stone Age, tribes buried their dead curled up like newborn babies. Scientists believe that this was done to prepare the dead for their coming rebirth. Ancient Egyptians believed that the dead are reborn as "some other living thing then coming to birth." Only after passing through creatures great and small is the spirit reborn in a human body. This "round trip," the priests said, takes three thousand years.

Math students study the work of Pythagoras, who lived in ancient Greece. Back in 500 B.C., Pythagoras was thinking about more than geometry. He claimed past lives as a warrior, a fisherman, and as the son of a god. Another Greek thinker carried this idea a step further. Plato believed that each person is born into one of nine levels of being. He taught that right-thinking people move up, level by level. Those who lead wicked lives risk being reborn as animals. In ancient Rome, people believed that their ancestors lived on in the bodies of house snakes. They fed and pampered these strange pets.

Matching beliefs can be found in modern tribal cultures. In the Pimbwe tribe of Tanzania, diviners are called in when a child is born. The diviner's task is to find out which ancestor lives on in the newborn. Some American Indians listen to the babbling of infants. They are hoping to hear their ancestors speak to them. In parts of India, families kill a chicken when a baby is born. Then they pray that a dead relative will find a new life in the newborn. Australian Aborigines believe that grandparents are reborn in the bodies of their grandchildren.

Beliefs like these are not confined to tribal cultures. Many famous people have claimed that they can recall past lives. Napoleon Bonaparte, ruler of France in the early 1800s, believed he was born to conquer Europe. A thousand years before, he said, he had ruled as the

A family of Australian Aborigines poses for a photo. Aborigines believe that grandparents are reborn in the bodies of their grandchildren.

France's Emperor Napoleon Bonaparte (left) believed he was born to conquer Europe. A thousand years earlier, he told his people he had ruled as the Emperor Charlemagne (right).

great Emperor Charlemagne. In the early days of the United States, Benjamin Franklin wrote, "Finding myself to exist in the world, I believe I shall in some shape or other always exist. With all the [ills] human life is liable to, I shall not object to a new edition of mine. [I hope] however, that the [errors] of the last may be corrected."[1] The American author Henry David Thoreau echoed Franklin's beliefs. "As far back as I can remember," Thoreau said, "I have . . . referred to the experiences of a previous state of existence. . . . I lived in Judea eighteen hundred years ago. . . . As the stars looked to me when I was a shepherd . . . they look to me now as a New Englander."[2]

Two famous Americans, Benjamin Franklin (left) and Henry David Thoreau (right), each believed that he had lived many past lives.

A belief in past lives once helped change the path of a nation. During his childhood in the late 1800s, Homer Lea was troubled by strange dreams. In time, he realized that the people in his dreams were Chinese. The sounds he heard were war trumpets. Even though he was quite short and had a deformed spine, Lea prepared himself for a soldier's life.

At that time, China was in the midst of a rebellion. Lea recruited a small army and joined the fighting. Although the revolt failed, Lea's military skills brought him fame. Still driven by his vision, he joined forces with Sun Yat-sen. The two men led a second uprising that toppled the Manchu Dynasty. By the end of 1911, China had become a republic.

The Search for Bridey Murphy

An amateur hypnotist and a Colorado housewife made news in the 1950s. Morey Bernstein talked Virginia Tighe into trying age regression. Tighe was a willing subject. In her first session, she recalled events that dated back to her first birthday.

During the third session, Berstein took a bigger step. He told Tighe to go "back, back, back," to another time and place. After a pause, Tighe began to speak with an Irish accent. She said she was Bridey Murphy and that she lived with her father in Ireland. She said her birthday was December 20, 1798.

In later sessions, Bridey described her life in great detail. She talked about growing up, her marriage, and the details of everyday life. Tighe had never visited Ireland, but Bridey's knowledge of Irish customs and places was almost perfect. An 1801 map matched her description of the area around the Murphy cottage.

Bernstein turned the tape-recorded sessions into a book called *The Search for Bridey Murphy*. Some skeptics said that friends must have coached Tighe in the details of Bridey's life. Others said she learned her facts by watching films. Was Tighe a fake? No one ever proved that, though many made the claim. Sixty years later, the case of Bridey Murphy still inspires those who are eager to explore past lives.[3]

Virginia Tighe relaxes on a couch as she enters a hypnotic trance. During her age regression sessions, Tighe went back to Ireland in the eighteenth century and described her life as Bridey Murphy. Hypnotist Morey Bernstein, who tape-recorded Virginia's age regression, turned the tapes into a book called *The Search for Bridey Murphy*.

Until his death about a year later, Lea spoke of himself as a "man of destiny." Had he spent a past life in China? Lea could not say for sure. A Buddhist monk may have glimpsed the secret when he read Lea's palm. This is the hand of a king, the monk said.[4]

Did the monk truly see the life line of a dead Chinese ruler in Lea's palm? The facts can be argued both pro and con. But the impact of Lea's childhood dreams cannot be ignored.

Although he was American, Homer Lea dreamed that he had once lived a soldier's life in China. He gathered a force of men and traveled there to help lead the rebellion that toppled the Manchu Dynasty in 1911.

Glimpses
of a Distant Past

The year is 1918. A British soldier serving in France leaves camp to buy tobacco. As Alex Ainscough wanders through the old city of Rouen, he feels a sudden chill. The street seems so familiar! In his mind's eye, he sees himself marching with a line of soldiers. All are dressed in black armor. He knows they will soon view the burning body of Joan of Arc.

As quickly as it appeared, the vision fades. Back in his own time, Ainscough walks on until the street ends in a market square. A marker catches his eye. Its inscription gives him a second chill. It says that Joan of Arc was burned to death on that very spot.[1]

Ainscough guesses that he has experienced *déjà vu*. The French phrase means "already seen." Unlike an age regression, a sense of déjà vu seems to pop out of nowhere. Most often, people are visiting a new place. All at once they feel strongly that they have been there before.

A couple were driving through a German town neither had seen before. Suddenly, the woman pointed to a house. That's where I lived

Alex Ainscough stares at a marker stating that Joan of Arc was burned to death at this spot. Ainscough feels he's had a déjà vu experience. Moments earlier, he had seen himself marching with a line of soldiers to watch the burning of the warrior saint.

in a past life, she said. Her name, she went on, had been Maria D. Impressed by this strong sense of déjà vu, the couple stopped at the village inn. The husband asked the owner about Maria's family. All of them are dead, the man told him. Little Maria, he added, died after a horse kicked her. On hearing this, the woman broke down and cried. Through her tears, she described Maria's last, painful moments.[2]

Instinctive flashes are very closely related to déjà vu experiences. Someone walks into a room and instantly "knows" a secret about that room. A young woman, for example, was touring an English manor.

What happened to the doorway, she said, pointing at a blank wall. Old plans confirmed that there had been a doorway there, but it was now plastered over. In a similar case, an American stopped to see the ruins of Heidelberg Castle in Germany. As he toured the old castle, a thought flashed through his mind. There's a book hidden in a certain room, he told the castle guards. The room he described was closed to tourists. A search, however, turned up the long lost book.[3]

Memories of past lives often show up in dreams. A British woman, for example, was often troubled by a scary dream. In the dream, she and a playmate fall from a high balcony. Rushing toward them as they fall she sees a black-and-white tile floor. The dream did not make sense to the woman. Then she visited a house that was said to be haunted. She took one look at the tile floor and knew she had seen it before. A guide told her that two children had fallen to their deaths on that floor. Later, as she toured the house, the woman saw two portraits. Those people were my mother and father, she gasped. The guide said she was staring at paintings of the dead girl's parents.[4]

Some people who believe in past lives point to the lives of child prodigies. At five, Wolfgang Amadeus Mozart was writing classical music. "Blind Tom" Bethune was a black slave who lived in Georgia before the Civil War. When he was four years old, Tom touched a piano for the first time. The blind child was soon playing with great skill, the record says. Jean Cardiac, born in France in the 1700s, knew the alphabet at three months. By age six he could speak half a dozen languages.

A British woman is troubled by a recurring dream, in which she and a friend fall from a balcony. Then, on a visit to a haunted house, she sees the black-and-white tile floor from her dream. The tour guide tells her that two children once fell to their deaths on that floor.

Did these children learn their skills in an earlier life? Those who believe in past lives say there is no other way to explain their talents.[5]

Henry Ford, the automaker, welcomed the concept. Ford wrote, "Work is futile if we cannot utilize the experience we collect in one life in the next. When I discovered reincarnation, it was as if I had found a universal plan. . . . Some seem to think [genius] is a gift or talent, but it is the fruit of long experience in many lives."[6]

Some past-life memories seem to be triggered by illness or accident. A Connecticut doctor described an incident of this type in 1975. After raking leaves all morning, he sat down to rest. A moment later, his body began to shake. He felt as though he was falling down a long, black tunnel. When he finally emerged into the light, he was sitting in a

The Dorothy Eady Case

Dorothy Eady was three years old the day she fell down a flight of stairs. At first, her parents feared she was dead. Then, in what seemed a miracle, Dorothy opened her eyes. Aside from a few bruises, she escaped her fall without injury.

In the weeks that followed, Dorothy slept badly. In her dreams, she saw a temple and a garden unlike anything in her native England. Her parents did not know what to make of her new complaint. She missed her "real home," Dorothy said.

When she was older, Dorothy claimed that the Egypt of 1300 B.C. was her real home. She said she had been a priestess named Omm Sety. The pharaoh at that time was Sety I. Although sworn to purity, Omm Sety became the pharaoh's lover. Soon after—fearful that her secret would be revealed—she killed herself.

Dorothy was obsessed by her vivid memories. As an adult, she moved to a village near the ruins of Sety's temple. There, she renewed Omm Sety's ancient vows. At night, she told friends, she often left her body to visit her long-dead lover. She also kept herself pure. Doing so, she believed, would allow her to rejoin Sety after her own death.[7]

Dorothy Eady believed that she had been a priestess named Omm Sety in a previous life. Obsessed by her vivid memories, Eady moved to a village in Egypt near the ruins of Sety's temple and renewed her ancient vows.

well-furnished room. A servant entered and told him his horse was ready. The doctor rode into town, passing men on camels along the way. He went to a tavern to meet some friends. As the night wore on, a fight broke out. His last memory was of being kicked in the head. When he woke up he was back in his own yard.[8]

Was the doctor dreaming? Or did his fainting spell take him back in time? No one can answer those questions with any certainty. One fact, though, is clear. All over the globe, millions of people claim that they have caught a glimpse of past lives.

CHAPTER FOUR

Age Regression Under Hypnosis

Glenda H. put aside her doubts and stepped into Dr. Kay's office. She had been hypnotized before, but today was different. This time, Dr. Kay would use age regression to return her to a past life.

Dr. Kay welcomed Glenda warmly. "Medical hypnosis is perfectly safe," he assured her. "You won't turn into a zombie. In fact, you will be fully aware of everything that happens." Then he switched on his tape recorder. Glenda liked the idea that she could listen to the tape later on.

To start the session, Dr. Kay asked Glenda to lean back in her chair. She closed her eyes and breathed deeply. As she relaxed, Dr. Kay told her she would feel warmth spreading through her body. As his soft voice droned on, Glenda fell into a deep, sleeplike trance.

"You are moving back in time through a long, black tunnel," Dr. Kay said. "At the count of ten, you will be in a new time and place. Don't be surprised to find yourself in someone else's body. All that you see in that former life will be clear and vivid. When you hear my voice, you will respond to it."

As Dr. Kay counted to ten, Glenda remained calm. This was a relief. Some age regression subjects become upset and cry out. When she was ready, Dr. Kay asked, "What is your name?"

"My name is Clara Kincaid," Glenda told him. She said she was a milkmaid on a farm in southern England. The date, she thought, was around 1810. But given her lack of schooling, she could not be sure. Urged to go on, Clara said she was an orphan. A kind neighbor had given her shelter and work to do. Dr. Kay found her English accent hard to understand.

At first, Clara spoke as though she were watching a film. Then she began to describe the smells, tastes, and feelings of her simple life. She discussed her work as a milkmaid in great detail. Asked about her friends and family, she named a dozen people. Then she described each of them.

Clara Kincaid, Dr. Kay learned, had died at eighteen. Clara talked about her long illness and her foster mother's tears. To the doctor's surprise, she also told him about her own funeral. Afterward, she said, she traveled to a spirit world full of light and music.

Dr. Kay told his subject it was time to return. "You will remember all the details of your journey. You will feel relaxed and happy when you wake up," he added. Then he counted backward from ten. At zero, Glenda opened her eyes and smiled.

During a session of age regression, Dr. Kay tells Glenda that she's moving back in time "through a long, black tunnel." As Glenda's past-life visions become clear, she tells the hypnotist her name is Clara Kincaid, and she is a milkmaid on a farm in southern England.

A woman relaxes while undergoing hypnosis. During an age regression session, the hypnotist will help the subject recall details of a past life.

"Have you ever traveled to England or milked a cow?" Dr. Kay asked. "You just gave me a grand tour of an English dairy farm."

Glenda laughed. "In this life I'm a stay-at-home lab tech," she said. "As for cows, the closest I've been to one was at the county fair." Her answer did not surprise Dr. Kay. Subjects often describe distant lands and speak in strange accents during age regression.[1]

The Strange Case of Miss C

Hypnotic age regression has as many critics as it does supporters. The critics remind us that a hypnotized subject wants very much to please. What happens when the subject is told to talk about a past life? That person may reach into the unconscious for the details needed to create an imagined past life.

The case of Miss C seems to prove the point. Early in the 1900s, British researchers studied an amazing young woman. Miss C claimed to "remember" living as Blanche Poynings some five hundred years earlier. Her favorite food, she said, was eels stewed in oil. She also described her close friendship with Maud, Countess of Salisbury. Her detailed stories of life in the Middle Ages caused a sensation.

In a later session, Miss C mentioned a novel called *Countess Maud*. One look at the book cleared up the puzzle. Almost every detail of Miss C's story appears in the novel. When questioned, she admitted that she had read the book long ago. Unknown to her, the words had buried themselves in her unconscious. Under hypnosis, Miss C's unconscious mind had supplied the details for the fictional Blanche.[2]

As Glenda stood up and stretched, Dr. Kay gave her a few words of caution. Never try age regression without the aid of a trained hypnotist, he said. Amateurs often expose their subjects to injury. Then he told Glenda about a Los Angeles nurse named Doris Williams.

Williams had always wondered about her fear of deep water. During age regression in 1979, she returned to a past life as Stephen Blackwell.

The young man, she claimed, had been a passenger on the *Titanic* when it sank in 1912. As she told the story, Williams showed signs of stress. Blackwell's wrists had been broken as the ship lunged upward, she said. Her own hands and wrists began to ache. The hypnotist relieved the pain by snapping her out of her trance.[3]

Glenda understood the serious warning. If the hypnotist had not acted quickly, Williams might have suffered a lasting injury.

Age regression with Dr. Kay was another matter. Did she really have a former life as a milkmaid? Glenda made up her mind. She would study both sides of the debate on age regression.

Passengers in lifeboats watch in dismay as the *Titanic* sinks in 1912. In 1979, during an age regression session, Doris Williams claimed that she had been Stephen Blackwell in a past life. She said Blackwell had been a passenger aboard the doomed ship.

Science Tackles the Question of Past Lives

Scientists feel safest when they can control each step of their research. Mix compounds A and B in a test tube. If done right, the mixture always smells like rotten eggs. The study of past lives cannot meet that standard. Most of the people who report past lives are sincere, researchers admit. Many past-life stories hold up when checked against the records. But what about Miss C and others like her? The chances for fraud are too great.

No one denies the tape-recorded accounts made during age regression sessions, but science looks for simple answers. Professor Ian Stevenson, a leader in the field, limited his studies to children. Adults, he says, feel they must respond when the hypnotist says, "Return to your past lives." Anxious to please, they make up tales using details drawn from the unconscious mind. Stevenson calls this process *cryptomnesia*.

Dr. Reima Kampman used age regression on a group of teenagers to test the theory of cryptomnesia. A teenage girl named Dorothy claimed to remember eight lives, including one from the Middle Ages in England. She even recited a popular song from the times. During a later session, however, Dorothy revealed that she had once read "The Cuckoo Song" while waiting at a bus stop. To Kampman, this discovery proved that her case was one of cryptomnesia.

A study by Finland's Dr. Reima Kampman seems to prove this theory. Kampman used hypnotic age regression with a group of teens. One thirteen-year-old girl, Dorothy, claimed she could remember eight lives. From ancient Babylon to World War I, she described each life in detail. One life that caught Dr. Kampman's ear was that of an innkeeper's daughter.

Dorothy said that she was born near Norwich, England, in the Middle Ages. Her knowledge of place-names and events checked out exactly. Most amazing of all, the girl sang what she called the "Summer Song." The words, research showed, came from a rare piece of music known as "The Cuckoo Song." Was this proof of a past life? This girl knew only a few words of English. Yet here she was, singing words few had heard for hundreds of years.

The puzzle was not solved until Kampman ran a new study seven years later. After he hypnotized the girl again, he asked her about the "Summer Song." This time the girl told him of the day she had taken some books from the library. While waiting for a bus, she had paged through *The Story of Music*. A quick glance at a page from "The Cuckoo Song" had been enough to store it in her unconscious. Months later, the song surfaced again as part of Dorothy's "past life." Kampman concluded that this was a clear case of cryptomnesia.[1]

Dr. Stevenson also has doubts about adult age regression. However, he trusts the "memories" that children report. Roberta Morgan, for example, scolded her mother for not being like her "other mother." When shown a new food, Roberta would say, "I had that lots of times.

Linking Past and Present: Birthmarks and Phobias

The *Journal of Nervous and Mental Diseases* ran an offbeat article in 1977. People with past-life memories, Dr. Ian Stevenson wrote, often have phobias or birthmarks. These "scars," he found, were linked to the person's death in an earlier life.

One child recalled a death by drowning. She fell from a bridge after she jumped back to let a bus go past. In her present life, the girl feared bridges, buses, and water. Bath time was a kicking, screaming ordeal in her house. It took four adults to hold her in the bathtub.

Birthmarks, Dr. Stevenson found, are proof of wounds suffered in a past life. An Indian named Ravi Shankar was born with a line that circled his neck. The birthmark, he said, was left from a past life in which he had been beheaded. Another child told of being shot in a past life. He had a birthmark on his chin that could have been the entry wound. His scalp showed a second mark. That mark could have been the exit wound.

Do children make up past-life stories to explain their fears and birthmarks? Dr. Stevenson checked the stories against hospital records. In each case, someone by the same name had died in the way described by his subject.[2]

Don't you remember?" So how do these distant memories surface? Dr. Stevenson does not know. He speaks about a psychophore, or a "vehicle," that carries memories from one life to another. The old body, he suggests, becomes a model for the new.[3]

Some researchers use genetics to explain memories of past lives. Human genes, they claim, may carry memory traces in their DNA.

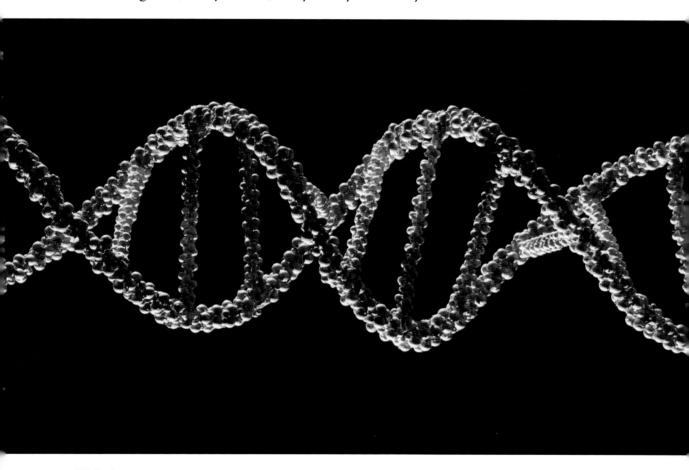

This is a computer-generated model of DNA. Some researchers claim that human genes may carry memory traces as part of their DNA. Perhaps this is the mechanism that enables people to recall past lives.

After all, instincts such as sucking and a fear of falling are present at birth. The Swiss psychologist Carl Jung long ago claimed that humans are born with racial memories. Jung said, "The mere fact that people talk about rebirth . . . means that a store of psychic experiences described by the term must exist." Jung also admitted that "rebirth is not a process that we can in any way observe. We can neither measure nor weigh or photograph it."[4]

A third theory of past lives depends on a belief in extrasensory perception (ESP). Telepaths, for example, seem to read minds at a distance. Clairvoyants claim they can track down killers by touching the victim's clothes. Could Doris Williams have used ESP to relive Stephen Blackwell's death on the *Titanic*? Critics say no to this theory, too. Show us, they say, a link between the two. One died before the other was born. They did not share a common family, birthplace, or lifestyle. Further, they note, even gifted telepaths do not claim contact with the dead.

Despite the skeptics, people go on exploring past lives. Most of us, after all, have had a déjà vu experience or two. And for some folks, belief in past lives offers hope for the future. If you believe you have lived before, it is easy to believe you may live again.

Why Stop With the Past?

Sigmund Freud has been called the founder of modern psychology. His insights into the causes of mental illness have helped millions of people. Many problems, he taught, are linked to the long-ago events of childhood.

Herman is a normal teenager—except for his phobic fear of horses. What causes that fear? Buried in Herman's mind, Freud would say, is a bad memory linked to a horse. Until Herman deals with that long-buried incident, his fear will rule his life.

Dr. Helen Wambach took Freud's ideas a step further. She developed a system called Past Lives Therapy (PLT). If Herman came to her for help, she would take him back to childhood under hypnosis. Once there, she would ask him to talk about horses. Did a pony kick Herman when he was a baby? Recalling the accident would alert Herman to the cause of his fear.

What if Herman had never been hurt by a horse? Wambach would ask him to go back even further. Somewhere in a past life, she would say, lies the root of the problem. Perhaps Herman was trampled to death

Herman has a phobic fear of horses. According to Sigmund Freud, his fear could be related to a bad memory involving a horse. In order to overcome his fear, Herman must come to terms with that repressed memory.

while working on a ranch. If so, he would be asked to relive his death on that long-ago day. Knowing the source of his fear would help him conquer it.

Past life therapists say that anyone who can be hypnotized can be helped. The International Association for Regression Research & Therapies, Inc. (IARRT) in Riverside, California, is a center for this work. Dr. Wambach once surveyed over 18,000 IARRT patients. More than 90 percent said they had regressed to one or more past lives. Most claimed that the treatment helped them solve their problems. Reliving their deaths in a past life did not upset them.

Before she died in 1985, Wambach worked with more than one thousand patients. Some described past lives dating back to 2000 B.C. Her data showed that 49.6 percent had been women and 50.4 percent were men. Only a few enjoyed lives spent as kings or queens. Most said they had been farmers or manual laborers. Their reports of clothing, foods, and events matched the history books. Did W.N. mention a gold coin used in ancient Greece? Wambach could almost always find its twin in a coin book.[1]

As the work went on, Dr. Wambach noticed an odd fact. While in a sleeplike state, some patients seemed to become telepaths. To her surprise, they sometimes answered questions before she asked them. If that was true, she asked herself, could they look into a more distant future? Could she "progress" her patients instead of regressing them?

Dr. Wambach put her volunteers into a trance. Then she took them forward, year by year. "It's the Christmas season ten years from now," she would say. "You find yourself in a grocery store. Go over to the meat counter. . . . Tell me, what is the price of a package of pork chops?"

Dr. Helen Wambach worked with more than a thousand patients using Past Lives Therapy (PLT). Some patients described lives dating back to ancient times. Most said they were manual laborers and farmers, such as the man depicted here in this ancient Egyptian hieroglyph (top). Only a few claimed to have been kings or queens. Is it possible that you or someone you know was Queen Elizabeth in a past life?

Dr. Wambach put her patients into trances that had them look toward the future. One patient, Chet Snow, saw doomsday coming before the year 2000. His visions, of course, did not come to pass. Even so, doomsday still provides a popular theme for science-fiction television, books, and movies. This photo shows a scene from *The Book of Eli*, starring Denzel Washington (right), in which the world has turned cold and dark, just as Chet Snow said it would.

Most of her subjects gave detailed reports of life in the near-future. The price of food showed a steady rise, they claimed. Then, as they neared the year 2000, her subjects reported a sudden sense of release. Dr. Wambach believed that she knew what that meant. They had lived through their own death.

A vision of a possible future took shape. It appears that drought and storms will cause crops to fail. The globe will be rocked by earthquakes. To compound the disasters, nations will fight for scarce food supplies. In the United States, survivors will hide out on farms and ranches. Chet Snow, for instance, saw himself living in the desert. A bitter wind chills

Will humans be forced to abandon Earth sometime in the twenty-second century? Some of Dr. Wambach's **PLT** patients foresaw a day when people would be forced to take refuge in futuristic space stations like this one.

him to the bone. He and his friends gather to eat porridge from an iron pot. It is a cold, dark day in 1998, he tells Dr. Wambach. We now know that Chet's visions were not the least bit accurate. No doomsday has yet occurred.

Chet also had visions about the 2100s. He saw people living under the shelter of great, huge domes. He said back-to-nature colonies would sprout in plush, garden-like settings. A second group will take the leap into outer space. Some of these pioneers will live and work on space stations. Spaceships will carry settlers to Venus and Mars. The voyagers will dress in jumpsuits and clump about in magnetic boots. Supper will consist of bland-tasting food cubes. Contact with UFO's will become common.[2]

How accurate are these forecasts? Given the failure of his earlier predictions, you cannot put much trust in Chet's visions for the next century. Dr. Wambach's coworkers said that other subjects from the United States, France, and Russia told similar stories. Only time can prove or disprove their faith in these reports. Clearly, research is still probing the depths of the human mind. No one can predict what wonders will be uncovered. Perhaps past-life regression—and future progression—will one day be common events.

Chapter Notes

Chapter 1. "Daddy, I'm Coming Home"

1. Ian Stevenson, *Children Who Remember Previous Lives* (Charlottesville, Va.: University Press of Virginia, 1987), pp. 55–57.

2. Ibid., pp. 80–84.

Chapter 2. A Belief That Spans the Ages

1. Sylvia Cranston and Carey Williams, *Reincarnation* (New York: Julian Press, 1984), p. 19.

2. Ibid., p. 23.

3. John Fairley and Simon Welfare, *Arthur C. Clarke's World of Strange Powers* (New York: G. P. Putnam's Sons, 1984), pp. 224–225.

4. Dumas Malone, *Dictionary of American Biography* (New York: Charles Scribner's Sons, 1933), vol. VI, pp. 69–70.

Chapter 3. Glimpses of a Distant Past

1. John Fairley and Simon Welfare, *Arthur C. Clarke's World of Strange Powers* (New York: G. P. Putnam's Sons, 1984), p. 226.

2. Stuart Holroyd, *Psychic Voyages* (Garden City, N.Y.: Doubleday, 1977), pp. 137–138.

3. Interview with a psychic, Lomita, Calif., August 1992.

4. Ibid.

5. Editors of Time-Life, *Psychic Voyages* (Alexandria, Va.: Time-Life Books, 1987), pp. 122–123.

6. Sylvia Cranston and Carey Williams, *Reincarnation* (New York: Julian Press, 1984), p. 333.

7. Rosemary Ellen Guiley, *Harper's Encyclopedia of Mystical & Paranormal Experience* (New York: HarperCollins, 1991), p. 433.

8. From the authors' files.

Chapter 4. Age Regression Under Hypnosis

1. Edith Fiore, *You Have Been Here Before* (New York: Coward, McCann & Geoghegan, 1978), pp. 20–25.

2. Rosemary Ellen Guiley, *Harper's Encyclopedia of Mystical & Paranormal Experience* (New York: HarperCollins, 1991), p. 433.

3. Laile Bartlett, *Psi Trek* (New York: McGraw-Hill, 1981), pp. 264–266.

Chapter 5. Science Tackles the Question of Past Lives

1. John Fairley and Simon Welfare, *Arthur C. Clarke's World of Strange Powers* (New York: G. P. Putnam's Sons, 1984), pp. 227–229.

2. Sylvia Cranston and Carey Williams, *Reincarnation* (New York: Julian Press, 1984), pp. 64–68.

3. Ian Stevenson, *Children Who Remember Previous Lives* (Charlottesville, Va.: University Press of Virginia, 1987), pp. 76–79.

4. C. G. Jung, *Memories, Dreams, Reflections* (New York: Vintage Books, 1989), pp. 318–319.

Chapter 6. Why Stop With the Past?

1. Rosemary Ellen Guiley, *Harper's Encyclopedia of Mystical & Paranormal Experience* (New York: HarperCollins, 1991), pp. 434–436.

2. Chet Snow, *Mass Dreams of the Future* (New York: McGraw-Hill, 1989), pp. 1–2, 39–40, 116–124.

Glossary

age regression—To move back in time to discover past lives, often under hypnosis.

ancestors—The men and women from whom a person is descended.

Brahmin—In a Hindu society, a member of the highest social and economic caste. Caste members live by strict rules regarding marriage, diet, occupations, and social contacts.

child prodigy—A young child who displays extraordinary talents or powers.

cryptomnesia—The retrieval of memories that have been buried in the unconscious mind. Subjects are not aware that they have been exposed to the data contained in these memories.

déjà vu—The feeling of having already been in a certain place or a certain situation, even though you know that is not possible.

diviner—A psychic who can reveal hidden knowledge.

DNA—The cells of all living things have a chemical substance called deoxyribonucleic acid (DNA). It contains the instructions for the cell's growth, reproduction, and all other activities.

extrasensory perception (ESP)—The general ability to send or receive information without using the normal senses.

hypnosis—A sleeplike condition in which the subject will accept almost any suggestion made by the hypnotist.

instinctive flash—A sudden sense of knowing that something is true, even though you cannot pinpoint the source of the feeling.

Past Lives Therapy (PLT)—A treatment in which hypnotists use age regression to help patients trace current life problems to past-life traumas.

phobia—A fear of a specific thing or situation, such as a phobic fear of heights or spiders.

psychophore—Dr. Ian Stevenson's name for the "vehicle" that conveys a person's past-life memories.

racial memory—Carl Jung's theory that babies are born with certain memories that are common to all humans.

reincarnation—The belief that one can be reborn in a new body or as a different form of life.

skeptic—Someone who questions widely held beliefs or theories.

unconscious mind—The storehouse of feelings, thoughts, and memories that the mind keeps hidden. If past-life memories do exist, they are apparently stored in the unconscious mind.

Further Reading

Books

Austin, Joanne P. *ESP, Psychokinesis, and Psychics*. New York: Chelsea House Publishers, 2008.

Herbst, Judith. *Beyond the Grave*. Minneapolis, Minn.: Lerner Publications Co., 2005.

Noyes, Deborah. *Encyclopedia of the End: Mysterious Death in Fact, Fancy, Folklore, and More*. Boston: Houghton Mifflin, 2008.

Parks, Peggy J. *ESP*. San Diego, Calif.: ReferencePoint Press, 2008.

Rooney, Anne. *Messages From Beyond*. Mankato, Minn.: Smart Apple Media, 2010.

Rosen, Marvin. *Meditation and Hypnosis*. Philadelphia: Chelsea House Publishers, 2006.

Internet Addresses

eHow.com: How to Discover Your Past Lives
<http://www.ehow.com/how_2276725_discover-past-lives.html>

How Stuff Works: How Déjà Vu Works
<http://science.howstuffworks.com/science-vs-myth/extrasensory-perceptions/deja-vu.htm>

The Skeptic's Dictionary: Past Life Regression
<http://www.skepdic.com/pastlife.html>

Index